This is Katie.
Katie grows vegetables in her garden.

1

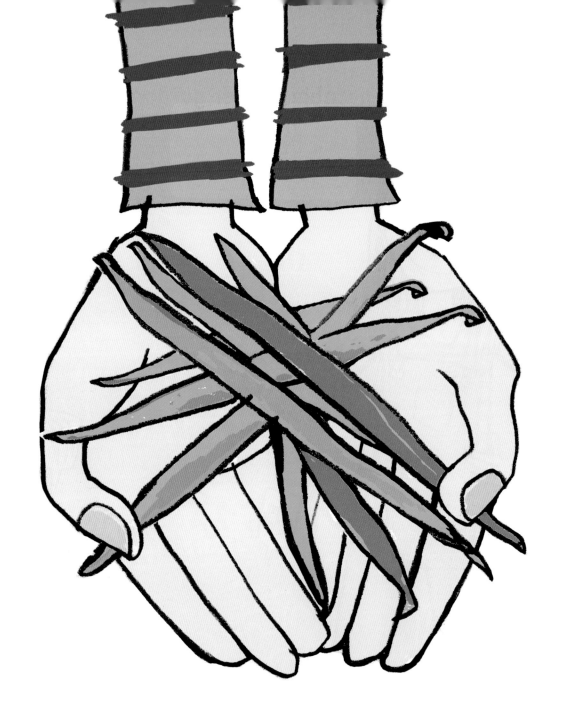

Katie likes beans.
They are her favourite vegetables.

Katie grows a bean plant.

She gets a small jar.

jar

Katie gets some tissue paper and a bean seed.

She puts some water and tissue paper in the jar.

Katie puts the bean seed in the jar.

She gives the seed some water and sunlight.
It grows!

It has got some roots and a stem.

It has got leaves. Now it is a bean plant.

Katie puts some soil in a big pot.

soil

She puts the bean plant in the pot.

Katie gives the plant some water.

It grows flowers!

Now there are beans on the plant!

Activities

Before You Read

1 Match the words and pictures.

bean seed   jar   pot   tissue paper   roots   stem   soil

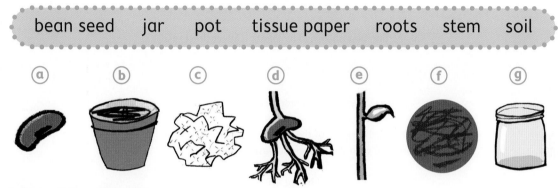

After You Read

1 Read and say Yes or No.

   a Katie does not like beans.

   b Katie has got a small jar and a big pot.

   c Katie gives the bean seed some milk.

   d The bean plant grows and grows.

2 Look at the pictures. Write 1, 2, 3, 4 or 5.

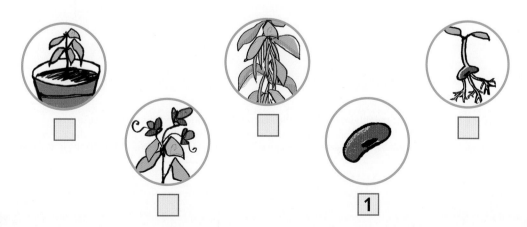

Pearson Education Limited
Edinburgh Gate, Harlow,
Essex CM20 2JE, England
and Associated Companies throughout the world.

ISBN: 978-1-4082-8823-8

This edition first published by Pearson Education Ltd 2013

10

Text copyright © Pearson Education Ltd 2013

The moral rights of the author have been asserted
in accordance with the Copyright Designs and Patents Act 1988

Set in 19/23pt OT Fiendstar
Printed in China
SWTC/10

Acknowledgements
Illustrations: Anna Hymas (Meiklejohn and New Division)

For a complete list of the titles available in the Pearson English Kids Readers series, please go to
www.pearsonenglishkidsreaders.com. Alternatively, write to your local Pearson Education office or to
Pearson English Readers Marketing Department, Pearson Education, Edinburgh Gate, Harlow, Essex CM202JE, England.